GIUSEPPINA ZIZZO

Photographs by
SANDRO and PAOLO DA RE

Translated into English by Ulisse Belotti

THE STORY OF THE BASILICA
OF SANTA MARIA MAGGIORE
IN BERGAMO

GRAFICA E ARTE BERGAMO

Previous page: *the Basilica seen from 'Piazza dell'Ateneo' (a print dating 1830), Bergamo Civic Library.*
Below: *northern portal seen from the portico of 'Palazzo della Ragione'; on the right 'Cappella Colleoni' (Colleoni's Chapel).*

CHRONOLOGY

XIIth-Century

Its foundation stone was laid in **1137** in local historians' opinion and in **1157** according to the most recent interpretation of local records.

1187: the building was not finished yet.

1194/95: the southern portal was mentioned for the first time.

XIIIth-Century

1248: the 'regio', a porticoed public space by the north wall of the transept was mentioned.

1273/79: the soldiers's portico, seat of the town army, located on the ground where 'Cappella Colleoni' (Colleoni's Chapel) stands, was mentioned.

XIVth-Century

1336: *The Virgin and the Child with Saints*, was frescoed in the south-western apse; this fresco is similar to *St. Alexander riding a horse*, discovered in '59 under the canvas by Zanchi and now placed in one of the women's gallery.

1340: the Baptistry was built; it was originally located at the end of the central nave; now it is in 'Piazza Duomo' ('Duomo' Square).

1347: *St. Bonaventura's Tree*, was frescoed on the southern wall of the transept.

1350: the massive wooden Cross was placed in the presbytery.

1351/53: the northern portal was built by Giovanni da Campione.

1360: the southern portal was built by Giovanni da Campione, in 1403 the spire by Anex de Alemania was added.

1367: the small north-eastern portal was built by Giovanni da Campione and his son Nicolino.

1375/90: Pacino da Nova frescoed *Events of the Virgin's life* and *The Last Judgement* in the central apse; in the same period were painted the two Virgins with the Child and Saints and *The Worship of the Magi* in the south-western apse and in the northern part of the transept, *St. Eligio, The Last Supper* and a few votive frescoes.

1389/92: Andreolo de' Bianchi made

The belfry and the dome of the Basilica; the dome of 'Cappella Colleoni' in the foregrund.

Left: *the façade of the 'Ateneo' and the central apse of the Basilica.*
Below: *the pronaos of the 'Duomo' seen from the northern portal of the Basilica.*

Above: *the apse of Santa Maria Maggiore in a print by Elia Fornoni (1880).*

Following page: *the northern portal. In the lower loggias is the equestrian statue of St. Alexander with Saint Barnaba and Proiettizio on each side; in the upper aedicula, the Virgin with Child between Saints Esteria and Grata.*

the procession-cross; it was stolen in 1973.

XVth-Century

1425/27: Giovanni da Campione started the construction of the belfry again; the work was carried on between 1436 and 1450 by architect Bertolasio Moroni and finished in 1591 with the copper spire.

1475: the soldiers' portico and the old

vestry were pulled down in order to build Colleoni's Chapel

1485/91: the new vestry was built by Giovanni Carrara from Serina and Simone Sirtori.

XVIth-Century

1514: Antonio Boselli paintend on canvas *Christ among Saints and Angels,* in the chapel on the right of the High Altar).

1521: the south-western portal was built by Pietro Isabello (the lunette, by Previtali, dates back to 1514).

1522/55: Lorenzo Lotto gives the cartoons for the tarsias of the choir which was inlaid by Gianfrancesco Capoferri and carved by Alessandro Belli.

1576: the changing of the interior began according to the suggestions of architects Martino Bassi and Pellegrino

Left: *a detail of the northern portal.*

Below: *northern portal, decorations of the arch.*

Tibaldi. The stucco-works were made by the lombard artists Francesco Brembilla and Della Porta.

1583/86: the nine Florentine tapestries depicting *Event of the Virgin's life*, were woven by Benedetto Squilli according to Alessandro Allori's cartoons.

1584: Gian Paolo Lolmo painted *The Virgin and Child with Saints Rocco and Sebastiano*, in the north-eastern apse.

1585: Gian Paolo Lolmo painted *The Harvest of manna*, on canvas, in the south-eastern apse.

1586: Gian Paolo painted *The bronze serpent in the desert*, on canvas, in the north-eastern apse.
Francesco Bassano painted *The Last Supper*, on canvas in the south-eastern apse.

1589: Gian Paolo Cavagna painted *John the Evangelist*, on canvas in the chapel

on the left of the High Altar.

1591/1602: the two pulpits were built; the former by Giuseppe Prepositi according to Lorenzo Della Porta's design, the latter similar to the previous one, by Antonio Salvetti and Alvise Zanardi.

1592: Francesco Bassano painted on canvas the four ovals of the presbytery vault depicting 'Events of the Virgin's

Life' (*Birth, Presentation, Annunciation, Visitation*).

1593: Gian Paolo Cavagna painted on stone *The Assumption*, in the bowl of the apse and *The worship of the Magi*, on the left side of the choir.

1594: Gian Paolo Cavagna painted *Esther* and *Judith*, on canvas in the presbytery.

1595: Enea Salmeggia, named 'il Talpino' painted *The Workship of the Magi*, on canvas, on the left side of the choir.

1596: Camillo Procaccino painted on canvas *The Apostles discovering the Virgin's empty grave*, in the choir.

1597 / 98: Camillo Rizzetto made the six bronze candlesticks.

XVIIth-Century

1614: the dome was modified according to Binago and Richino designs.

1615: a competition was held in order to decorate the dome; Francesco Zucco, 'il Talpino' and Cavagna took part in the competition, each of them with an angel frescoed on an oval; Cavagna won the competition and was entrusted with the task of painting the *Coronation of the Virgin* and eleven *angels* in the dome, besides the ten *Prophets* of the tambour.

Below: *detail of the apse; on the right the 'Ateneo'.*
Right: *windows and the practicable gallery of the central apse.*

1627: Flemish tapestries depicting *Vespasian's triumph* were bought and placed on the organs.

1651/58: Fra' Massimo da Verona painted *The Slaughter of the Innocents*, on canvas, on the right wall of the southern part of the transept.

1651/94: stucco-works by Sala brothers from Lugano.

1656: Pietro Magno painted on canvas *Moses and the miraculous water*, in the south vault of the transept.

Johann Cristophorus Storer painted on canvas *Moses with the Tables of the Law*, in the south vault of the transept.

1657: Ottavio Cocchi painted on canvas *Jacob and Rachel*, *The Creator*, *Isaac's Sacrifice*, *Rebecca*, *Jacob's staircase*, in the south vault of the transept.

1658: Giovanni Dart painted *Isaac and Abimelec*, on canvas in the south vault of the transept.

1659: Luigi Scaramuzza painted *David and Goliath*, on canvas, in the south vault

14

Detail of the small apse by the belfry.

of the transept.

Giuseppe Nuvolone painted *Abel's death*, in the south vault of the transept. Gian Paolo Recchi painted *Adam and Eve* and *Moses taking off sandals*, in the south vault of the transept.

1661: Pietro Liberi painted on canvas *The Deluge*, on the front of the southern side of the transept.

1665/67: Ciro Ferri painted on canvas: *God cursing the serpent, The harvest*

of manna, Esther and Ahasuerus, The Creator, Moses saved by the waters, Ruth Abigail quieting David, David with a harp, Michel and the dragon, Samuel introduced to Elijah, Gideon, Jacob fighting with the Angel, Flijah and Acab on Mount Carmel* in the north vault of the transept.

1670: Antonio Zanchi painted on canvas *Moses and the miraculous water*, in the northern side of the transept.

1678: Federico Cervelli painted *Noah's sacrifice after the Deluge*, on canvas, on

the left wall of the northern side of the transept.

1681: Luca Giordano painted on canvas *The Pharaoh flooded by the waters*, on the wall at the bottom.

1692/94: Nicolò Malinconico painted on canvas: *Abraham and the three Angels, The Defeat of Jericho, Jacob and Rachel, Joshua stopping the sun, Angels, David holding Goliath head, Deborah' the Prophetess, Judah the Maccabean attacking Datema, Samson and the lion, Angels, Balthasar's banquet, Balaam and the old age, Elijah's kidnapping, Manoe's*

Previous page: *southern portal with the ornamental spire.*
Below: *coping of the southern portal and detail of the coping.*

*Gothic spire above the
southern portal.*

sacrifice, *Samson's father,* in the vault of the nave and *The Immaculate Conception* and *Joseph with the Angels,* below the choir.

1696/98: the Flemish tapestries, depicting the*Crucefixion,* woven by Johannes Reghelbrugghe and designed by Ludwig van Schoor, were bought along with *The Immaculate Conception,* and *Moses in the burning bramblebush,* below the choir, besides those, were bought or given the thirteen sixteenth-century Flemish tapestries depicting various subjects.

XVIIIth-Century
1770/73: Giuseppe Alari made the inner doors of the two main portals with statues by Giuseppe Sanz.

XIXth-Century
1802/33: the High Altar was built according to Leopoldo Pollack's designs and with bass-reliefs by A. M. Pizzi and Grazioso Rusca.

1839: the monument to Cardinal Longhi, by Ugo da Campione, once in St. Francis Monastery (Concento di S. Francesco) was placed in the right aisle.

1852: Innocenzo Fraccaroli carved the

monument to Simone Mayr, at the end of the nave.

1855: Vincenzo Vela carved the monument to Gaetano Donizetti, at the end of the nave.

1899: the confessional by Andrea Fantoni and his workshop was bought (left aisle).

XXth-Century
1915: the massive organ by Vegezzi-Bossi was bought. A few frescoes, painting were restored as well as the exterior.

19

Right and following page: *detail of the southern portal.*

THE LOCATION

The Basilica stands in the centre of the old town but has it been always there? No doubt about it, particularly if you consider the town-planning and the history of Bergamo.

S. Maria Maggiore was built in the XIIth-century on the ground upon which a smaller church, devoted to the Virgin, stood, and its construction went on in the XIIIth-century.

From a historical point of view, the centuries in which the Basilica was re-built were particularly important to Bergamo; as regards home politics, the episcopal government was replaced by a municipal government in which the nobles held office.

Besides this, people asked they could take part in the running of the political and administrative life of the town. As regards foreign politics, it was the period of the Lombard League against

Friedrich Barbarossa, not to mention a series of minor wars against Brescia and the riots caused by Guelphs and Ghibellines. The building and the development of the Basilica seem to be strictly linked with the citizens' self-consciousness; the Basilica has always been a reference point to them: S. Maria was the church the Bergamaschi preferred. This is the reason why they never stopped taking care of the works of art and buying new ones. Local historians handed down that the Basilica was erected by the inhabitants of Bergamo in order to be released by a vow made to the Virgin because of a plague. No matter of it is true or not; what matters is that this is a clear evidence that the church was extremely popular, being named either 'Chapel of the town' or 'basilica of the vow', in order to state it as central in the civil and religious life of Bergamo.

From the town-planning point of view, the ground on which the church was built, had always been the most important part of the town from either political or religious point of view: on the same area was located the Roman Forum with its civil and religious buildings; it was right here that the episcopal government, either in the Cathedral or in St. Vincent's palace, used to hold office. Inside the central area, the Church carried out a central role from the very beginning: in its 'regio' (sort of large portico standing on the site of the present northern portal with the wall of the ancient local units of measurement) Bergamaschi used to be in session for resolutions; below the north-western portico, the so-called 'porticus militum', which does not exist any more, used to meet 'The Society of S. Maria Maggiore', 400 armed men who were the town army, under the orders of the head of the Commune.

Left: *the square of the 'Duomo'.*
The Basilica of Santa Maria Maggiore is on the left.

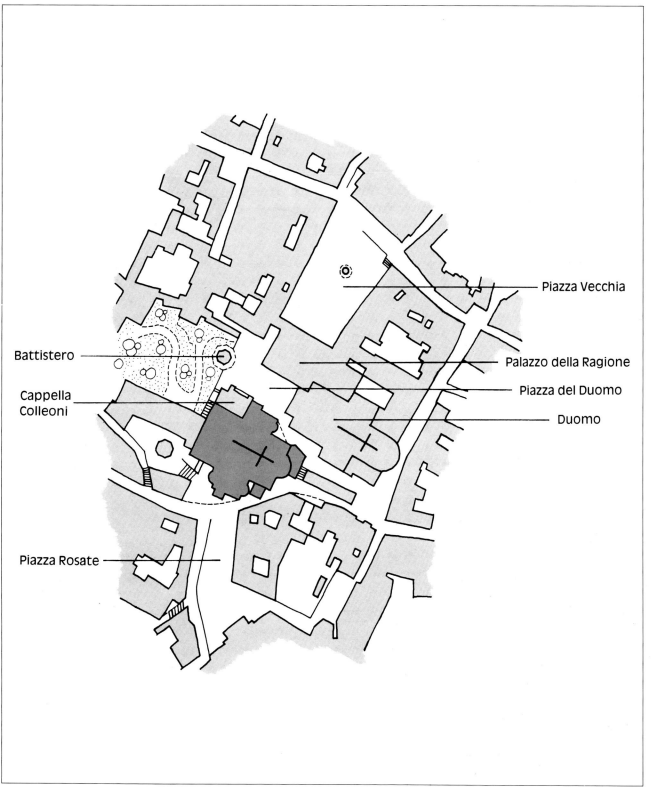

Piazza Vecchia

Battistero

Palazzo della Ragione

Piazza del Duomo

Cappella
Colleoni

Duomo

Piazza Rosate

Detail of the northern transept.

Above: *detail of the dome.*
Below: *interior of the Basilica.*

Lots of citizens used to keep their valuables in chests, placed in the Basilica itself, which may be considered as real 'banks'. This testifies, one more time, the central role of the Basilica in the public and private life of the Bergamaschi; even the location of the approach roads testifies its central feature. The main entries are situated on the north-south axis, not on the east-west one, as it is customery in any church, so you walk from one side to the other without directing your steps straight to the Altar, as the traditional architecture suggests. The north-south axis links the square of the 'Duomo' with 'Piazza Rosate' (Rosate Square), named square of 'Antescolis' in communal times, two important squares for the town economy. The Church was probably erected on the road which linked the two squares, so that the Basilica could be of service either to passers-by hurrying for business or to those who wished to meditate or pray.

The anomalous location of S. Maria Maggiore, compared with other churches of the town, was officially confirmed in 1449, when the Church was run by 'Consorzio della Misericordia', a group of laymen whose aims were charitable works and mystical practice together with various cultural activities and in 1453 when the Basilica, owing to Pope Nicolò V's bull, was exempted from the episcopal jurisdiction.

Left: *the Altar seen from the wooden choir.*
Following page: *in the presbytery.*

The front of the presbytery.

CHORVS

THE ERECTION

The building of the basilica started towards the half of the XIIth-century, when Romanesque period was at its best, yet different influences coming from various area and cultures testify the cultural liveliness of this building even if located in a small province town. The Church is on the plan of a Greek cross with several apses, four of which can be seen outside and three inside the Church; the small north-western apse was pulled down at the end of the XVth-century in order to erect 'Cappella Colleoni' (Colleoni's Chapel); the small south-western apse is now walled up inside. Such a plan, unusual in western countries, comes from plans of Greek cross which developed and proliferated in Balcan countries.

The walls show some details which clarify the original events of the Church, built in two different periods; first the eastern side and a part of the transept, later the western side. The two different stages are clearly visible because of the way the sanstone blocks were used; large and squared during the first stage, small and irregular during the second one. The structure of the apses reflects the changing economic situation: the three eastern apses; erected during the 'rich stage', are more accurate and elegant in proportions and decorations; the western one is poorer in decorations. The plan of the apses, with two orders having the former a floor with splayed windows and the latter a floor

Below: *pulpits and candlesticks.*

Architectonic Chronology

1137. The Basilica was started (1157 according to recent researches). 1340. The baptistry (now situated opposite the 'Duomo') was built at the end of the nave. 1351-53. Northern portal (A). 1360. Southern portal (E). 1367. Small northeastern portal (B). 1525-27. The works for erecting the belfry started again (it was finished in 1591) (D). 1475. The old vestry was pulled down in order to erect 'Cappella Colleoni' (Colleoni's Chapel) (G). 1485-91. New vestry (C). 1521. Small south-western portal (F). 1576. They started modifying the interior. 1614. The dome was modified (H).

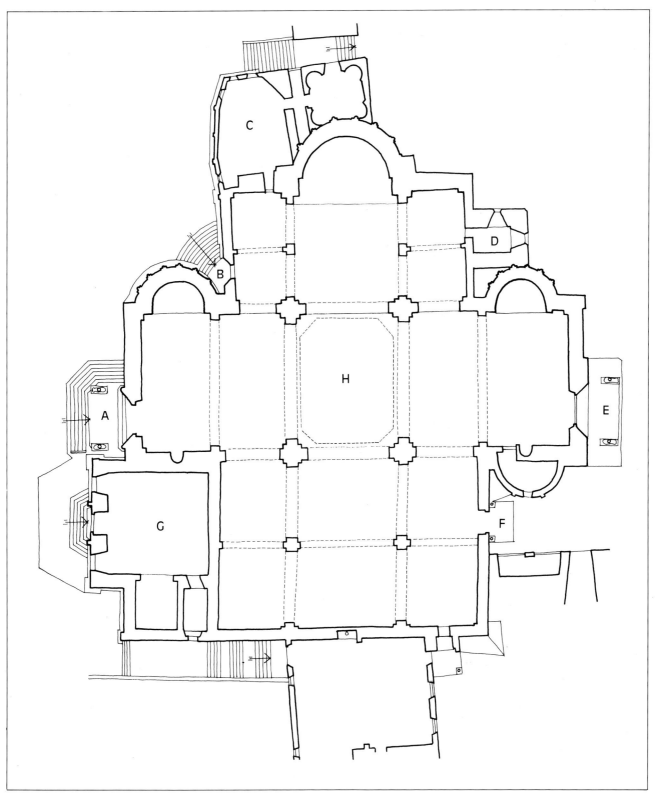

"The crossing of the Red Sea", a tarsia based on Lorenzo Lotto's design.

"Noah's ark", a tarsia based on Lorenzo Lotto's design.

34

Previous page: above *"Judith and Holofernes"*, below *"David and Goliath"*, two tarsias based on Lorenzo Lotto's designs.

Right: *the wooden cross of the presbytery.*
Below: *tarsias of the choir.*

with a practicable gallery, comes from Lombardy and developed later in the Rhine area.

The dome, where the transept crosses the nave, has an irregular octagonal plan and it is composed of three galleries sloping down; the first having round arch windows, the second and the third having mullioned windows; because of the slenderness of its proportions it can be compared with a contemporary Rhine dome being both built before cuspidated towers which were often built in Lombardy in the Gothic period. A series of half-covered spaces were added outside (XII-XIIIth centuries), along with courts and porticoes, where peo-ple used to talk business or even argue. The interior of the Church was divided into two parts: the nave and the aisles, the transept and the presbytery with the main chapel and the small side chapels on the lower floor; the women's gallery, in the believers' area and in the preists' area on the upper floor. These rooms can be reached only through a maze of staircases and routes winding in the hollow space exsisting between the outer wall and the inner wall; a com-plicated system which links outer and women's galleries, attics and the dome. The interior looks different nowadays if compared with the massive original structure and this is due to the changes occurred in Manneristic and Baroque times. From the end of XVIth-century and throughout the XVIIth-century, the vaults were stuccoed, the women's gal-leries walled up and the original columns coated with Corinthian pilaster strips. We do not know the reason why these changes were made; some say that the Basilica was unsteady (it is clear that these changes made it steadier); others say that the reason was merely aesthetic (the interior of the most popular Church of Bergamo was completely redecora-ted according to a new taste). What mat-ters is that the Basilica can be considered as the result of a pleasant misture of different styles.

Left: *the octagonal dome.*
Below: *left choir, ''Worship of the Magi'', a canvas by Talpino.*

THE DECORATION

Towards the mid-XIIIth-century, the structure was ready to be filled: with the XIVth-century starts the story of the decoration of S. maria Maggiore; a long and rich story. From a chronological point of view, starting from the artists and the works they made, we can identify a first stage, from XIIth to XVth century, when the Church is Lombard without any doubt, an intermediate stage, in the XVIth-century, influenced by Venetian and Tuscan art and a final stage, from XVIIth to XIXth century, influenced by national and European art, from Milan and Venice to Rome and Neaples, from the Ticino river area to Flanders.

If we consider, on the contrary, the decoration according to an artistic point of view, that is painting, sculpture and minor arts, we can not but note the richness in quantity and quality of each section, bearing in mind, at the same time, the guiding thread that links different ages and techniques, that is the presentation and exaltation of the Virgin in her prefigurations (Esther, Judith...), events of her personal life (Birth, Presentation in the Temple, Annunciation, marriage, Death, Assumption, Coronation) and in relationship with Christ (the worship of the Magi and sheperds, Verginity and Immaculate Conception, Crucefixion). In addition there are several paintings depicting events from the Old and New Testament but a complete iconological exam has not been made yet.

Anyway the decoration of S. Maria Maggiore will not cease amazing thanks to the munificent patronage of the people who ran the Basilica. As regards the paintings, we have a fourteenth-century stage of which important parts still remain; the two walls of the transept and others that can not be seen because located in rooms not open to the public, the small south-western apse and the women's gallery linked with the apse itself, and other which are lost but mentioned in the records and some experts are still discussing to decide whether they were located in the main apse (in the lower part behind the stalls of the choir and in the upper part, behind Procaccini's canvas). In '500 the 'Presidenti della Misericordia' (The Basilica Council) entrusted local artists with the task of decorating the Basilica; for example Boselli (from S. Giovanni Bianco, 1470-1532), whose Lombard taste mingled with Venetian influences; Lolmo (1550 - 1595) whose ancientness and simplicity went well with the Counter-reformation, Cavagna (Bergamo 1556-1627) and Talpino (1565 ab. - 1626), the main representatives of late Bergamasque '500, both representing Classicism but with different aspects; a Venetian painter, Francesco Bassano (Bassano 1549-1592) was involved with painting depicting pastoral and biblical events and a Bolognese painter, Camillo Procaccini (Bologna 1550 - Milan 1629), influenced by Milanese culture.

In '600 the 'Misericordia' Council promo-

1. 2 - Gian Paolo Lolmo: *The Virgin and the Child with Saints Rocco and Sebastian, 1584; The bronze serpent in the desert, 1586.*   **3 -** Gian Paolo Cavagna: *St. John the Evangelist, 1589.*   **4. 5. 6. 7 -** Francesco da Ponte (Bassano): *Events of the Virgin's Life: Birth; Presentation; Annunciation; Visitation respectively, 1592.*   **8. 9. 10 -** Gian Paolo Cavagna: *The Assumpion, 1593; Esther and Judith respectively, 1594.*   **11 -** Camillo Procaccini: *The Apostles by the Virgin's grave, 1596.*   **12 -** Antonio Boselli: *Christ among Saints and Angels, 1514.*   **13 -** Francesco da Ponte: *The Last Supper, 1586.*   **14 -** Gian Paolo Lolmo: *The Harvest of manna, 1585.*   **15 -** Gian Paolo Cavagna: *The worship of the sheperds, 1593.*   **16 -** Enea Salmeggia (Talpino): *The worship of the Magi, 1595.*   **17 -** Gian Paolo Cavagna: *The Coronation of the Virgin, 1615.*   **18 -** Francesco Zucco: *Angel, 1615.*   **19 -** Enea Salmeggia (?): *Angels, 1615.*   **20 -** Gian Paolo Cavagna and son: *Angels, 1615-1616.*   **21 -** Gian Paolo Cavagna and son: *Prophets, 1615-1616.*   **22. 23. 24. 25. 26. -** Ottavio Cocchi: *Rebecca; Isaac's Sacrifice; The Creator (in the oval); Jacob's staircase; Jacob and Rachel respectively, 1657.*   **27 -** Cristophorus Storer: *Moses with the Tables of the Law, 1656.*   **28 -** Pietro Magno: *Moses and the miraculous water, 1656.*   **29 -** Fra Massimo da Verona: *The Massacre of the Innocents, 1657-1658.*   **30 -** Giovanni Dart: *Isaac and Abimelec, 1658.*   **31 -** Giuseppe Nuvolone: *Abel's death, 1659.*   **32 -** Gian Paolo Recchi: *Adam and Eve driven out of the garden of Eden, 1659.*   **33 -** Gian Paolo Recchi: *Moses taking off sandals, 1659.*   **34 -** Luigi Scaramuzza: *David and Goliath, 1659.*   **35 -** Uncertain (Scaramuzza?): *Glaele stabbing Sisara's temples, 1660.*   **36 -** Pietro Liberi: *The Deluge, 1661.*

37. 38. 39. 40. 41. 42. 43 - Ciro Ferri: *God cursing the serpent; David with a harp;Moses saved by the waters; The Creator (in the oval); Abigail quieting David; Ruth; The harvest of manna; respectively, 1665-1667.*   **44. 45. 46. 47. 48. 49 -** Ciro Ferri: *Esther and Ahasuerus; Elijah and Acab on Mount Carmel; Samuel introduced to Elijah; Michel and the dragon (in the octagon); Jacob fighting with the angel; Gideon; respectively, 1665-1667.*   **50 -** Antonio Zanchi: *Moses and the miraculous water, 1670.*   **51 -** Federico Cervelli: *Noah's sacrifice after the deluge, 1678.* **52 -** Luca Giordano: *The Pharaoh flooded by the waters, 1681.*   **53. 54. 55. 56. 57. 58. 59 -** Nicolò Malinconico: *David holding Goliath's head; Deborah the prophetess; Angels (in the oval); Samson and the lion; Joshua stopping the sun; Judah the Maccabean attacking Datema; respectively, 1692-1694.*   **60. 61. 62. 63. 64. 65. 66 -** Nicolò Malinconico: *Balthasar's banquet, The Defeat of Jericho; Balaam and the old age; Angels (in the oval); The Sacrife of Manoe; Samson's father; Jacob and Rachel; Elijah's kidnapping; 1692-1694. The two paintings hanging from the old choir depicting 'Immaculate Conception' and ''Joseph with the angel'' are by* Malinconico *as well.*

Captions by Mons. Prof. A. Meli.

Detail of the dome.

Following pages: *"St. Bonaventura's tree" (1347), a fresco in the southern transept.*

'The Pharaoh being flooded' by Luca Giordano.

ted an ambitious decorative enterprise aiming at including artists from all Italian schools. Starting from Milanese school with Gian Paolo Recchi (Borgovico 1600 ab. - 1683), one of Morazzone's followers, with Johann Cristophorus Storer (Costanza 1611 - Milan 1671) born in Switzerland but brought up in Lombardy where he painted most of his works with Giuseppe Nuvolone (Milan 1619-1703). The Venetian school has the most representatives; among them, Frà Massimo da Verona (Verona 1607-1679); a nostalgic of Veronese and Tintoretto's art.; Pietro Liberi (Padua 1614 - Venice 1687), one of the most famous Venetian Baroque artist; Federico Cervelli (Milan 1625 - Venice 1700 ab.), whose

VENERA[...]
DE BAIA[...]
MINOR[...]
IN SACRA[...]
QVI POS[...]
ROMANA[...]
SVA OPER[...]
QVO PVLC[...]
OMNIVM[...]
ET DECO[...]
VETERIS[...]
DÑS GV[...]
ORNATV[...]
DEPINGE[...]

Above: "St. Bonaventura's tree", detail of the fresco. Middle: details of "The Last Supper" and below, St. Antonio Abate, a Saint Apostle, Virgin and Child and other votive frescoes. Following page: the fourteenth-century frescoes on the northern wall of the transept; among them "The Last Supper" and "St. Eligio's story".

first known work is housed in the Basilica; he was a versatile painter thanks to his smoothness of style and his creative talent; Antonio Zanchi (Este 1621-1722), with his dramatic violence and violent light and shade and Giovanni Dart who worked mainly in Treviso during the second half of seventeenth century. The Emilian school is represented by Luigi Scaramuzza (Perugia 1616 - Milan 1680) who is considered 'Emilian' either because he was one of Guido Reni's followers or because he was great-

ly influenced by Guercino who was asked to paint in the Basilica but they did not come to an angreement. The Roman school is represented by Ciro Ferri (Rome 1634-1689), one of Pietro da Cortona's followers and the Neapolitan one is represented by Luca Giordano (Neaples 1634-1705), called 'the speedy' because of his speed in painting (some say ironically becuase of his way of painting, that is with quick and essential strokes) and Nicolò Malinconico (Neaples 1663-1721), one of Luca Giordano's followers;

he was recommended to the 'Misericordia' by the master himself, so that he could be entrusted with the work of finishing the decoration of the Basilica.

The same variety of periods and styles can be found out in the sculptures as well even if they seem to be more uniform; as a matter of fact all the sculptors came from Lombardy; some of them were unknown but filled apses and women's galleries with decorations

47

depicting flowers and animals.
Giovanni da Campione, the artist who designed and made the portals, used to sign his works of art, which is typical of Gothic artists.
Lombard was Ugo da Campione, the sculptor of the monument to Cardinal Longhi and Lombard are the stucco-works as well as the artist who designed the phantasmagoric confessional which was carved in walnut and boxwood by Andrea Fantoni; the confessional can be considered a theological summary of the Confession; Lombard were the two nineteenth-century masters, Innocenzo Fraccaroli and Vincenzo Vela, who made the monuments to Simone Mayr and Gaetano Donizetti.
In the Basilica you can also admire several examples of the so called 'minor arts' such as the Flemish and Florentine tapestries, being the latter ones of the series coming from Florence which remained where originally set or cabinet-works such as the choir, which is a mixture of carvings and inlaid works.

Above: *interior of the small south-estern apse.*

Following page: *south-western apse, frescoes depicting St. Cristoforo, a Saint martyr, Virgin on the throne, a saint monk protecting the offerer and Henry, the saint emperor of Saxony (1336).*

HOCOPUS FECIT FIGVRARE ... ... DIE ... ... MILLESIMO ... CENTESIMO ... ...

49

The Basilica owned a precious work of jewellery, a processional cross by Andreolo de' Bianchi, a fourteenth-century architect-sculptor, but it was stolen in 1973.

The decorations of S. Maria Maggiore show the principles which inspired those who commissioned the Church and those who built it. In the northern portal, for example, along with images of bishops and abbots, are carved soldiers and hunters; in the southern portal, if on the left panel five saints are portrayed and Christ and the Apostles on those of the front, on the right panels stone-cutters and carvers at work are portrayed: that is to say that not only sacred images are worth being portrayed in a religious building but also images of work and everyday life. This is the reason why tapestries were chosen to decorate the walls; tapestries used to be hung in castles and mansions, seldom in religious buildings.

The way the choir was set is unique for its kinds; it is composed of stalls facing the altar in the shape of a U with right angles and stalls behind the altar, in the shape of a half-circle; the former being reserved to the religious of the Basilica such as the Prior, the Choir-master, the Sacristan, the Master of ceremonies, the Tutor of servers and chaplains, the latter being reserved to laymen, rectors, governor, administrator, doyens.

Below: *Florentine tapestry, "The Virgin's nuptial ceremony", according to Alessandro Allori's cartoons.*
Following page: *detail of the tapestry.*

Fleminsh tapestry on a wall at the end of the Basilica: "Crucefixion" according to Louis Van Schoor's cartoon.

GUIDED VISIT

A visit to a church should start from the façade, usually the visiting-card of a building; as a matter of fact S. Maria Maggiore never had a real façade but only side entries, two main entries and two minor entries. Joined to the western side of the Basilica, is a quadrangular hall, divided by a big arch and covered with fourteenth-century frescoes; in the wall which corresponds to the western side of the Church there is a mullioned window, now walled up, with frescoes depicting the first two Bishops of Bergamo: St. Narno and St. Viatore: the thirteenth-century style and decorative style is clear in them. Walking around the north-western, side, where 'Cappella Colleoni' stands, but where originally stood a small apse symmetric to the ones still remaining, you get to the northern front of the transept. The blocks of sandstone and the decorations, a serie of small wall-arcadings with a saw-toothed taenia, both Romanesque, were replaced by the massive portal by Campione which dates back to 1351-53. The portal is composed of a small portico with red marble columns ending with the traditional lions, here enriched with small lions- two tamers - a little dog biting the lion's tail; a small loggia with a three trilobated arches with the statues of St. Alexander riding a horse and St. Barnaba and St. Proiettizio; a niche with the statues of the Virgin and Child and the Bergamasque martyrs Grata and Esteria. The splay of the portal is rich in herring-bone and twisted mullions along with panels displaying head of religious or lay men or pastoral scenes. Walking on you get to the small north-eastern apse; in the lower part there is a series of splayed windows, now walled up, divided by shafts, with Corinthian capitals, in the middle a corona with geometric ornaments. In the upper part there is a practicable gallery, composed of spaces covered with barrel-vaults resting on corbels stuck in the wall and opened by round arches. The upper corona bears the same ornaments of the median one, being both the result of nineteenth-century repairs. In the north-eastern angle there is another portal by Giovanni da Campione, built in 1367 which seems to be poorer because of the material, sandstone, and

the decorations. The splay is composed of rosettes, dentils and small cubes; the corona with an ogee arch is enriched with volutes and angels stretching towards the Christ placed on the keystone having the Virgin and St. John on each side. The lunette, cut out and fitted, was made before the small portal and it depicts the *Nativity of the Virgin:* on each side St. Simeon and St. Joachim seem to peep from two half-open doors, in the middle two drawn curtains show the main scene; on the left St. Lucy and St. Anastasia washing the baby and on the right St. Elizabeth and St. Susan helping St. Anne, mother, grandmother and puerpera respectively. Then you get to the vestry which is supported by a base composed of small trilobated arches containing liturgical vessels; the building has two orders: the surface of

the former is characterized by a series of pilaster strips with Corinthian capitals, enclosing rectangular windows supported by voluted corbels; the latter is completely smooth with a large window, right in the middle of the main side. The central apse, as well as the small south-eastern and south-western apses, has the same structure of the small north-eastern apse; the mouldings of the central apse are original as well as the upper one which is saw-toothed and in the shape of small palms, and the one in the south-eastern apse with images of animals and plants. Now we get to the southern portal, composed of a small portico supported by columns ending with white marble lions and pilasters lying on kneeling telamones; the decoration was made with the panels already mentioned. The small portico

Inside tour

a. Monument to Cardinal Guglielmo Longhi (XIVth-century); it was moved here from St. Francis Convent when it was closed. **b.** Monument to Simone Mayr, a musician who was one of Donizetti's masters (1852). **c.** "The Crucefixion", a Flemish tapestry (1696-98); above: "The Pharaoh being flooded", by Luca Giordano (1681). **d.** Gaetano Donizetti's grave, monument by Vincenzo Vela (1855). **e.** The confessional Andrea Fantoni made in 1705 for the 'Duomo' and placed in this church in 1899. **f.** Fourteenth-century frescoes ("The Last Supper"; "St. Eligio"). **g.** The small north-eastern apse; altar-piece: "Virgin and Child and Saints Rocco and Sebastian" by Gian Paolo Lolmo (1584). **h.** Sixteenth-century choir, designed by Bernardo Zenale; the tarsias were made in 1522-55 according to Lorenzo Lotto's suggestions. **i.** Small south-eastern apse; altar-piece: "The Last Supper", by Francesco Bassano (1586). **l.** "St. Bonaventura's tree", a fresco dating to 1347.

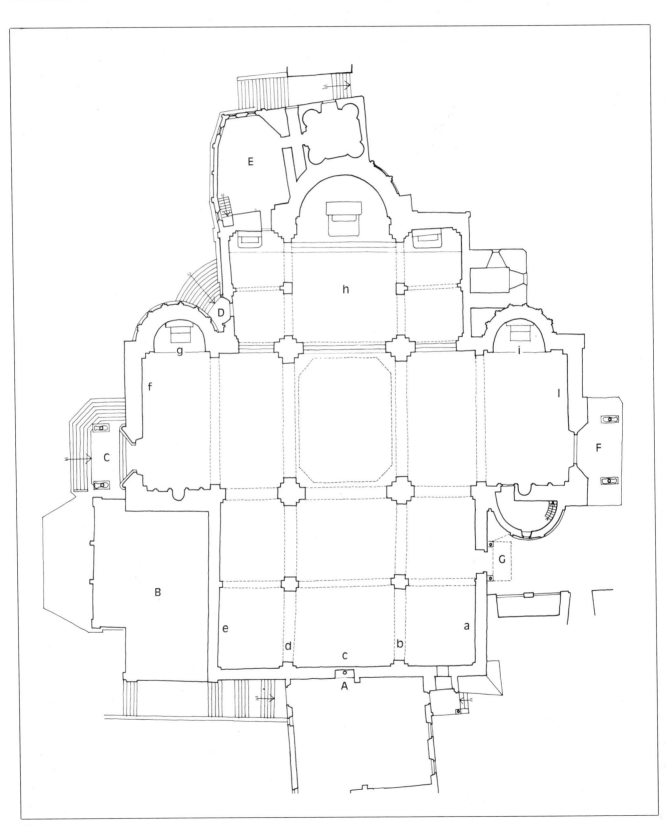

Outside tour

A. Walled up mullioned window with a XIIIth-century fresco (Saints Narno and Viatore, first bishops of Bergamo); this is the side where the façade originally stood; now it is linked with the Bishop's see. **B.** Colleoni's Chapel (XVth-century). **C.** The northern portal with three orders by Giovanni da Campione (1351-53); the statue of St. Alexander between Saints Barnaba and Proiettizio. **D.** Portal by Giovanni da Campione (1367); "Nativity of the Virgin" in the lunette. **E.** Vestry by Bramante (1485-91). **F.** Southern portal by Giovanni da Campione (1360); Gothic spire built at the beginning of the fifteenth-century. **G.** Portal by Bergamasque architect Pietro Isabello (1521).

Below: *monument by Vincenzo Vela on Gaetano Donizetti's grave.*

Monument to Cardinal Guglielmo Longhi.

was finished at the beginning of 15th century, by adding a slender spire, similar to the ones you can see on Milan 'Duomo'; some say that the architect who designed it, came from that building site. The small south-western apse, which is simpler in decorations and materials divides the portal by Campione and the Renaissance portal by Pietro Isabello, a local architect who was often mistaken for another or split into two. The result was that he was cheated out of some of his works or attributed works he had never made. When he designed this portal he wished to link with the portals by Campione, trying to renew them according to a renaissance taste; the barrel vault of the portal reminds the two small portals designed by Giovanni da Campione but this one is different because of the semplicity and elegance of lines; the vault, decorated with small rose-windows, is supported by two corbels decorated with valutes lying on two columns on each side of the wooden door.

Here is the entry to the Basilica; the interior is large and shady, in the shape of a Greek cross, it has a nave and two aisles, a marked transept and a deep presbytery. Leaving out the description of the paintings, whose authors and titles are mentioned in the chronology, we start our clock-wise tour from the end of the Church to the high altar. First we see the funeral monument to Cardinal Longhi which was moved here after closing St. Francis Convent where the munument was previously placed. The work is unanimously attributed to Ugo da Campione who, on designing it drew his ispiration from the Verona small portals and sarcophagi: a space with Gothic barrel vault lying on two sitting telamones and containing a sarcophagus supported by two small lions squatting down; their threesided heads display the mystic Lamb in the middle and two lions rampant on the other side. On the sarcophagus, the Cardinal's lean body is guarded by two deacons and two angels. On this side, besides the painting by Giordano and the tapestry depicting the 'Crucefixion', there are two funeral munuments: one to Simone Mayr, a Bavarian musician, and the other to his follower, Gaetano Donizetti. The Basilica, according to the function of 'civic' Church houses the mortal remains of Donizetti, one of the most famous man of Bergamo, celebrating him

through the symbols of the monument itself: in the bass-reliefs of the base there are seven puttos representing the notes of the scale; they are complaining and crying while breaking their instruments because of the death of the master. On the base there is also a woman, the Music, tormented and miserable. Walking on, you get to the massive confessional made by Fantoni, bought in 1898 by 'Consorzio della Misericordia' (the Basilica Council) from the parish of Zandobbio, where it was carried soon after it was made for the 'Duomo' of Bergamo.

It was the penitentiary of the 'Duomo', a canon named Mazza, who entrusted Andrea Fantoni and his workshop with the work, stating the ichonography which could be defined as a teological summary of Penance. Along the structure of the confessional, the artist placed the statue of God on the cyma, that

Below: *detail of the monument to Cardinal Guglielmo Longhi.*

Below: *Hall of the Bishop's see, linked with a wall of the Basilica, having a walled up millioned window.*

of the Misericordia with open arms, that of Wisdom with 'The Book' in her hands, that of Meekness with the Lamb in her arms, that of Silence; on the lower part that of Penance, the woman with veiled face and a cross, that of Disdain of the world, the strong man with a foot on the globe drawing the curtain on both sides of the opening; the bass-reliefs depict respectively: *The handing of the keys to St. Peter* on upper front panel, *The Resurrection of the son of* *Naim's widow* on the small door, *The Flagellation* and *The Deposition, The Justice* and *The Misericordia* on the small inside shutters and *Moses making water spring* on the back. If you stand opposite the High Altar, you are right in the front of the entry to the huge sixtennth-century choir which was designed by Zenale; the tarsias, one of the most important part of the choir, were made by Capoferri according to Lorenzo Lotto's cartoons. The choir is di- vided into two parts, being the former a half-circle round the altar and divided by two side-entries, forming the latter two mirror Ls on each side of the main entry; the stall are simple in structure in order to emphasize the tarsias which are the backs of the stalls. They display events of the Old Testament, as well as the four big panels at the entry of the choir, the ones which can be seen more easily. They are still in perfect condition thanks to the four covers Lotto himself

had planned; on them are symbols which refer to the stories they cover. The other tarsias were also planned to have covers but, further to a decision of the Council after their execution, the storied tarsias were placed on the backs of the laic part of the choir and the covers on the backs of the religious part, that on the front). The four tarsias at the entry represent: *The Pharaoh being flooded, Noah's ark, Judith and Holofernes, David and Goliath* respectively.

OPEN QUESTIONS

*T*his book about S. Maria Maggiore is either a historic-artistic guide to the building or a summary of what we know about it and what local critics and historians have written on it. Anyway this book can not be considered as a turning point of the researches on the Basilica but it is a sort of sieve between what has already been written and what will be written in the future. First of all a research is to be carried out in the records of 'Consorzio della Misericordia'; these records should give the most correct story of the Basilica from a chronological point of view and detailed news concerning the Basilica; this work seems to be very important but it has not been done yet. As regards the periods, starting from the Romanesque one, there is the problem of dating: according to a new hypothesis, based on records, the erection of the Basilica started in 1157 and this is contradictory to the age-old tradition, based on narrative sources, that is local historians who follow Jacopo Filippo Foresti's chronicle, and on the inscription which is on the arch of the southern portal. This inscription was carved in our century only, following another inscription previously painted and copy of the original one. Still to be answered are the questions concening the fourteenth-century frescoes, the sixteenth and seventennth-century paintings, the iconological reading of the wooden tarsias of the choir.

Worth mentioning are the recent studies on 'Cappella Musicale' of S. Maria which boasts of an important tradition; it was founded to support the services in the Basilica and it had such a development that it created, in the nineteenth-century, the present conservatoire. Maurizio Padoan has written a study on the music in S. Maria Maggiore during the first 30 years of the seventeenth-century giving advance notice of two researches: one, by Padoan himself, on the remaining years of XVIIth-century and one by Alberto Colzani, on the development of 'Cappella Musicale' from the origin to the sixteenth-century.

Above: *the women's gallery situated above the southern aisle.*
Below: *"Saint Cavalier", maybe St. Alexander, a fresco in the women's gallery.*

Following page: *the equestrian statue of St. Alexander by Giovanni da Campione, detail of the loggia of the northern portal.*

ESSENTIAL BIBLIOGRAPHY

A. PINETTI, *Cronistoria artistica di S. Maria Maggiore - Il Battistero,* in Bergomum, XIX, 4, 1925, pp. 167-183.

A. PINETTI, *Cronistoria artistica di S. Maria Maggiore - II: i portali, il campanile, la sagrestia nuova,* in Bergomum, I NS, 3, 1926, pp. 139-156.

A. PINETTI, *Cronistoria artistica di S. Maria Maggiore - III: l'interno nei secoli XIV-XV: gli affreschi,* in Bergomum, II parte II NS, 2, 1928, pp. 99-116.

A. PINETTI, *Cronistoria artistica di S. Maria Maggiore - IV: le curiose vicende di un'ancona di rame,* in Bergomum, II parte II NS, 3, 1928, pp. 131-151.

A. PINETTI, *Cronistoria artistica di S. Maria Maggiore - V: il coro ligneo di Gianfrancesco Capoferri e i disegni di Lorenzo Lotto per le tarsie,* in Bergomum, II parte II NS, 3, 1928, pp. 152-184.

G. DONATO-PETTENI, *L'Istituto Musicale G. Donizetti - La Cappella Musicale di S. Maria Maggiore - Il Museo Donizettiano,* Bergamo, 1928.

A. MELI, *Storia degli arazzi di S. Maria Maggiore in Bergamo,* Bergamo, 1962.

S. ANGELINI, *S. Maria Maggiore in Bergamo,* Istituto Italiano d'Arti Grafiche, Bergamo, 1968.

L. CHIODI, *Lettere inedite sulle tarsie di S. Maria Maggiore in Bergamo,* in Bergomum, LXII, 2, 1968, pp. 1-166.

G. ZIZZO, *S. Maria Maggiore di Bergamo 'Cappella della Città'. La basilica bergamasca nei secoli XII e XIII,* in Archivio Storico Bergamasco, II, 3, 1982, pp. 207-229.

F. CORTESI BOSCO, *"Et in una carta desegnato el coro con le quantità de le sedie da torno... per l'adaptar de le istorie",* in Notizie da Palazzo Albani, XII, 1-2, 1983, pp. 103-126.

©1984 Copyright by
GRAFICA E ARTE BERGAMO
Via Francesco Coghetti, 108
24100 Bergamo
Tel. 035/25.50.14

All rights of translation
and copy are reserved in
Italy and abroad.

Printed in Italy

The photographs were taken in 1984
by Sandro and Paolo Da Re
for the publisher only.

We wish to thank architect Vanni Zanella
for co-operating in the historic
and iconographic research,
architect Sandro Angelini and
Istituto Italiano d'Arti Grafiche
for permission to publish the pictures
on pages 1 - 6 - 14 - 40 - 41.

Layout
Emilio Agazzi

Paging
M. Grazia Taiocchi

Offset
Photo Offset, Bergamo

Photo-composition
GCF Ceriani, Bergamo

Printer
Istituto Grafico Litostampa, Gorle (Bergamo)

In quarto of cover: "Nativity of the Virgin", in the lunette of the north-eastern portal.